C000067123

Written by Elise Munier
Edited by Elizabeth Scoggins
Designed by Angie Allison

Picture Acknowledgements:

Michael Buckner/WireImage/Getty Images:
 front cover image, page 6;
Mike Marsland/WireImage/Getty Images:
 back cover image, page 29;
Peter Wafzig/Getty Images: pages 2–3, 9, 43, 62–63;
Ian West/PA Wire/Press Association Images: page 8;
Theo Kingma/Rex Features: pages 10, 15 (left and right);
Dominique Charriau/WireImage/Getty Images: page 11;
Frazer Harrison/Getty Images: page 12 (left);
Chris McGrath/Getty Images: page 12 (centre);
Matt Baron/BEI/Rex Features: page 12 (right);
Picture Perfect/Rex Features: page 13 (left);
Vince Flores/UK Press/Press Association Images:
 page 13 (centre);
Robert Pitts/LANDOV/Press Association Images:
 page 13 (right);
Irving Shuter/Getty Images: page 14;
Broadimage/Rex Features: page 16;
Ian Gavan/Getty Images: pages 19, 24, 44;
Christopher Polk/VF11/Getty Images for Vanity: page 20;
Rob Verhorst/Getty Images: page 25;

Chris McKay/WireImage/Getty Images: page 30;
Jason Merritt/Getty Images: pages 32–33;
Most Wanted/Rex Features: page 35;
Scott Gries/PictureGroup/EMPICS Entertainment/
 Press Association Images: pages 36 and 37;
Francois Durand/Getty Images: page 38 (left);
Stuart Wilson/Getty Images: page 38 (right);
Dave Hogan/Getty Images: page 39;
Kevin Winter/Getty Images: page 48;
Wong Maye-E/AP/Press Association Images/
 Press Association Images: page 51;
Sipa Press/Rex Features: page 54;
Michael Tullberg/Getty Images: page 57 (centre);
KPA/Zuma/Rex Features: page 58;
Jack Guez/AFP/Getty Images: page 59;
Agencia EFE/Rex Features: page 60;
ShutterStock Inc: images on pages 56, 57 (left and right),
58 (left); background graphics on pages 4, 5, 6–7, 10–11,
12–13, 14–15, 16–17, 18, 21, 24–25, 26–27, 28–29, 30–31, 34–35,
36–37, 38–39, 40–41, 42–43, 44–45, 46–47, 48–49, 50–51,
52–53, 54–55, 56–57, 58–59, 60–61.

Published in Great Britain in 2011 by Buster Books,
an imprint of Michael O'Mara Books Limited,
9 Lion Yard, Tremadoc Road, London SW4 7NQ
www.mombooks.com/busterbooks

Copyright © Buster Books 2011

All rights reserved. No part of this publication may be reproduced, stored in a retrieval system, or transmitted
by any means, without the prior permission in writing of the publisher, nor be otherwise circulated in any
form of binding or cover other than that in which it is published and without a similar condition including
this condition being imposed on the subsequent purchaser.
A CIP catalogue record for this book is available from the British Library.

ISBN: 978–1–907151–78–1

PLEASE NOTE: This book is not affiliated with or endorsed by Justin Bieber or any of his publishers or licensees.

1 3 5 7 9 10 8 6 4 2

This book was printed in July 2011 by L.E.G.O., Viale dell'Industria 2, 36100, Vicenza, Italy.

MIX
Paper from
responsible sources
FSC® C023419

By buying products with an FSC label you are supporting the growth of responsible forest management worldwide.
Papers used by Michael O'Mara Books are natural, recyclable products made from wood grown in sustainable
forests. The manufacturing processes conform to the environmental regulations of the country of origin.

JUSTIN BIEBER
ANNUAL 2012

UNAUTHORIZED

Ruby

Buster Books

CONTENTS

WELCOME TO JUSTIN'S WORLD!

Bieber Fever has swept the world, reaching millions of fabulous fans like you. With your help, Justin has gone from class clown to world-famous pop star in the blink of an eye!

A Shooting Star

Justin Bieber has always loved to sing, but his journey to stardom began when he was just 12 years old. Justin would sing around the house all the time, and he decided to enter a local competition, where he won third prize.

The Biebs didn't stop there — he also uploaded videos of himself singing to YouTube. Seven months and 10 million hits later, Scooter Braun, a managing executive from So So Def Recordings flew Justin and his mother to his offices in Atlanta. Not long after that, in October 2008, Justin signed a record deal with Island Records. The rest is history.

On his journey from small-town boy to international star, Justin has performed on stages all over the world. He's even starred in a documentary film about his life — *Justin Bieber: Never Say Never* — shown all over the world. His albums have sold millions of copies to adoring fans, and his tickets are quickly snatched up, making for tons of sold-out concerts.

What's next for this superstar? His life just keeps getting bigger and better, and this is only the beginning for J-Biebs.

Backstage Pass

This book is your VIP ticket to discovering the amazing world of the planet's hottest singer.

Not only can you get the inside scoop on his life before everyone knew his name (and copied his hairstyle), but you'll see how Justin's adjusting to life in the spotlight as one of the world's biggest stars. Read all about his most-recent superstar successes.

ALL THINGS BIEBER

Full name:
Justin Drew Bieber

Date of birth:
1 March 1994

Hair:
Brown

Eyes:
Brown

Nationality:
Canadian

Home town:
Stratford, Ontario, Canada

Lives:
Atlanta, Georgia, USA

★10★

Fave colour:
Purple

Fave foods:
Spaghetti bolognaise, cheesecake and 'Swedish Fish' sweets — also known as 'Big Foots'

Fave beverage:
Orange juice

Nicknames:
J–Biebs, JB, Biebs

Fave number:
6

Shoe size:
7.5

Idol:
Former _____ ____ player

Dream job:
Architect

Grade point average:
4.0

Pets:
A papillon dog called Sam

Funniest TV show:
The Inbetweeners

Hidden talents:
Can solve a Rubik's Cube in under a minute

Pet peeves:
When girls try to impress him, being asked his favourite _____ and being cold

Fave music video:
'Thriller' by Michael Jackson

Likes:
Apple pie

Really likes:
Girls

Dislikes:
Getting up in the morning

Fave coffee chain:
Tim Horton's

NEVER SAY ...

You might hang on his every word, but can you tell which Tweets are Justin's and who the others belong to? (There are some clues in the pictures below.) Check out page 61 for the answers.

1 Music is the universal language no matter the country we are born in or the color of our skin. Brings us all together

2 Last night was the end of my first tour! I couldn't have had a better time and I owe it all to you guys! Thank You!!! <3

3 Why do u drive on a parkway and park in the driveway. Its messed up

4 its about that time... RANDOM CHUCK NORRIS MOMENT: # Chuck Norris does not style his hair. It lays perfectly in place out of sheer terror.

5 Give the love you've got today it's the recipe for a better tomorrow

6 Got to rehearsal early. No one else is here yet. So......I'm in the production office making a necklace out of paper clips.

7 Tonights theme is... More is MORE!

8 having a moment. just grateful 2 b here living this life. not gonna waste the opportunity. not gonna be selfish. not gonna get in my own way

9 I'm so excited for the Oscars. Today someone asked me who I was wearing. Does anyone know who designed the Snuggie?

10 im not shaving for a month so you all can see my mustache.. im pumped

GROWING UP

Justin wasn't always standing in the spotlight and roaming the red carpet. Find out what it was like for the Biebs when he was growing up in Stratford, Ontario. From fishing trips to Christmas dinners and everything in between, get the scoop.

What a Catch

Justin was happy to get to spend time with his grandparents when he was growing up. One of his favourite memories is going fishing with them every summer at Star Lake in Canada. They would rent a cabin, and spend quiet mornings casting fishing lines out on the water. 'I hope someday I'll be out on Star Lake with my own grandkid, trout and telling

grandparents, grandchildren, stepgrandchildren, kids and stepkids — everyone was invited. Then everyone would settle down and eat a delicious turkey and gravy dinner. 'I'm telling you,' says Justin, 'my grandma puts up an awesome Christmas dinner.' After dinner, the gift-giving began. The whole family plays a game with dice to decide who gets which wrapped surprise. 'Then we all open our gifts and end up trading anyway,' Justin says.

Lucky Lad

Justin is truly grateful for his family. 'That's how we are in my family. Every person gives what they have,' says Justin. The down-to-earth star knows there is no such thing as a normal family, and he's glad his family aren't perfect. 'They'd

Justin Bieber

probably be the most boring people ever. Or the scariest,' he grins. Justin loves his family, and no matter how many family issues there may be, he wouldn't trade them for the world.

Meet the Parents

Bieber admires his parents — especially his mum for being a single mother, and being able to work and raise him 'a little prankster', as he calls himself. Definitely a family man, Justin is thankful for everything his parents have given him. 'My dad has influenced not only my life but my music,' Justin says. Even though his dad worked a lot, Justin loved spending time playing guitar with him and listening to classic rock.

Don't Mess with the Biebs

It seems unbelievable that anyone would pick on him now, but when Justin was in middle school, he was pretty short — even most of the girls were taller than he was! But Justin defended himself against bullies, mostly resolving things peacefully. One time Justin got sucked into a huge fight at school. 'I was never a big fighter,' Justin says. 'I preferred to compete on the basketball court or slice and dice them with my hockey skills.' He might prefer peace, but don't mess with this superstar! He says, 'I'm not a fighter by nature, but if I believe in something, I stand up for it.'

Class Clown

If Justin got in trouble for anything at school, it was usually for clowning around. He would play around on his skateboard, stir things up with his buddies or make someone laugh. But he never really got in trouble for being mean at school. 'Basically, I got in trouble for being myself, and that didn't seem fair to me,' says the Biebs.

AND THE WINNER IS

Justin may be only 17 years old, but he's already been nominated for and accepted several major music awards. He's lost some and won some, but there are definitely many more awards coming in the music star's bright future. Find out about the awards Justin has snatched up, and which ones he just missed.

Stratford Idol

In September 2007, Justin competed in a local talent competition in his hometown of Stratford, Ontario. He was just 12 years old, and had never been trained by a vocal coach like most of his fellow competitors. Still, Justin was able to win third place! 'I thought it would be a fun prize,' he admitted, 'but I was more into the idea of getting up in front of people and doing music just to see how it felt.' He admits that he was a bit crushed not to win at the time, but that he's glad for the way things worked out.

Gaga at the Grammies

In January 2010, Justin presented an award at the 52nd Annual Grammy Awards – along with fellow new artist Ke$ha. But at the 2011 Grammy Awards, Justin was nominated for not just one of the prestigious awards, but two! He says, 'All my life I have wanted to win a Grammy.'

Justin was nominated for Best New Artist and Best Pop Vocal Album, along with other superstars including Lady Gaga and Katy Perry. Unfortunately, Bieber lost out to Lady Gaga for Best Pop Vocal Album and to Best New Artist winner, Esperanza Spalding.

Even though the Biebs didn't sweep up any trophies this time, Esperanza Spalding says, 'He [Justin] was very gracious, and we met right after the show and exchanged hair touches. He was very sweet and gracious and he didn't seem upset. Very kind young man.'

The Junos

One of Canada's main music awards is the Junos. In 2010, Justin was nominated for New Artist of the Year, but he lost out to Canadian hip-hop star Drake. Justin wasn't giving up that easily though!

In 2011, he was nominated for a whopping four Juno awards and he took home the prize for Pop Album of the Year for *My World 2.0* and Fan Choice Award – the only category voted for by the public.

MuchMusic Awards

Another huge Canadian music award is the MuchMusic Award, which Miley Cyrus hosted in 2010. Out of four nominations Justin snagged both UR Fave New Artist and UR Fave Canadian Video. But he had two songs in the category of International Video of the Year by a Canadian, so JB beat himself when he won for 'One Time'. You can't win them all!

All That Glitters …

Justin is grateful for his success and loves to be nominated for awards. But he knows that awards and prizes aren't everything. 'Usher reminds me on a regular basis that there will be a whole lot of awards given out during the course of my career,' he says. 'It's an honor to be nominated and awesome to win, but you can't lose sight of the real honors and victories that happen off camera.'

MY WORDS

Get ready to do some serious searching! Ten words connected with Justin and his superstar world are hidden in the grid below and it's your job to find them. They could be going forwards, backwards, up, down or even diagonally. Check your answers on page 61.

Z	Y	G	O	S	O	S	B	F	G	J	Y	U	D	P
E	M	C	F	E	T	E	E	M	J	É	S	S	B	L
U	M	C	I	Q	Y	R	L	L	Q	L	J	M	Y	F
S	A	G	Y	O	S	T	A	P	E	O	X	I	B	H
A	R	P	N	E	J	J	E	T	Y	N	E	L	A	C
T	G	C	D	Z	N	H	L	G	F	G	A	E	B	O
H	É	R	E	T	T	I	W	T	A	O	I	N	J	O
Z	C	G	F	É	H	O	Q	B	L	Z	R	P	C	W
Q	S	D	Z	O	I	O	H	S	L	P	R	D	I	Q
L	Q	H	V	B	N	N	O	X	C	A	Z	J	W	V
D	O	P	Z	X	P	H	N	N	Y	O	K	I	H	Y
F	B	W	B	Q	Q	T	U	F	P	B	O	R	W	D
Z	H	Z	J	R	E	L	L	I	R	H	T	T	É	M
I	U	T	L	Q	I	W	F	F	F	O	H	T	E	M
Q	T	L	J	C	G	P	H	M	Q	Y	X	U	O	R

BABY
SELENA
BEYONCÉ
STRATFORD
GRAMMY
THRILLER
PRAY
TWITTER
SCOOTER
U SMILE

LOVE ME

Justin's cute smile and sweet songs go straight to the hearts of his adoring fans. But what about Justin and love? Get up-close-and-personal with the Biebs right here, and find out all about what goes on in his heart.

Ladies' Man

'I really like girls ... girls ... girls ... girls ... girls ... girls ... girls,' grins Justin. He's clearly a fan of the ladies, but what kind of girl is he looking for? As far as looks go, he admits that 'pretty eyes and a nice smile' are sure to turn his head. But that's not the most important thing for him. With his crazy, superstar lifestyle, the Biebs needs to be able to be a regular 17-year-old guy sometimes, so his favourite girl needs to be down-to-earth. Justin's also a legendary prankster, so a good sense of humour and the ability to make him laugh is a must.

Justin's heart doesn't flutter when girls wear loads of make-up to try and impress him. For him, it's all about letting natural beauty shine through. What's more, you don't have to be super-famous to win his heart. 'I would definitely date a fan,' says Justin with a smile. 'It would depend on the circumstances, but I don't rule out anybody.'

Love for the Fab Fans

Justin's worldwide army of devoted Biebettes are some of the most important people in his life. Every one of his fans is special to him, and Justin loves performing so he can connect with them. 'One of my favourite moments in every show is when I get to walk downstage, look right into those beautiful eyes and tell you, "If you need me, I'll come running from a thousand miles away ..."' he says. In 2011, he even decided to make each of his fans his Valentine on February 14th. Wow, what a heart-throb!

Dream Guy

If Justin picked you to be his date, you're sure to be one less lonely girl. Justin says his ideal night out would be to get something to eat, chat, and really get to know a girl. 'I hate being on a date where both people are working too hard to come up with stuff to say,' he says. 'You know it's working when you can just chill — listen to music, watch a movie or whatever — without feeling like you have to force the conversation. It should just be natural.'

After the first date's gone well, you can bet he'd make a wonderful boyfriend. At the Vanity Fair Oscars Party in 2011, Justin took to the red carpet with Disney starlet Selena Gomez. She looked beautiful in a long scarlet dress, and Justin had sweetly made sure his outfit matched his date's perfectly. He was looking super-suave in a tux, with a bright red handkerchief poking out of his jacket pocket.

So he's got attention to detail down, but what about some good old-fashioned romance? Justin was reportedly so smitten with Selena that he sent her enough bouquets of flowers to fill her house while he was away on tour. Awww!

Young at Heart

Justin says he's having a great time dating, and hanging out with girls, but he's definitely not ready to settle down yet. 'I think love is a learning process throughout your life,' he says. 'I'm still learning, I'm still trying to figure out girls!'

HAIR HE IS!

It's the look that gripped the world like extra-hold hairspray — the Justin Bieber hairstyle. Read on to find out all about those luscious locks.

Fantastic Flip

It wasn't just the original hair-do itself that caught fans' attention. Justin also had his adorable signature 'flip'. But why does he do it? Justin admits that he flips his sleek fringe out of his face with a simple head shake because his hair gets out of place. It must help him to see out from under all that hair, too!

More than Just a Haircut

Also known as the Twitch, Flip, Switch or Flow, the Bieber look became the hottest boy-style around. But surely it must have taken hours for JB to get his hair always looking so perfect? The Biebs confessed — 'After I shower,' he says, 'I blow dry my hair and just shake it and it goes like that.' That's hair-raisingly amazing!

Get the Look

Justin's trademark floppy locks have been a magnet for girls. The haircut must be really magical, as some boys have paid up to $175 to get the Bieber-look.

Trimming the Tresses

Early in 2011, Justin told MTV that he was thinking about cutting his hair a bit shorter after the premiere of his film, *Never Say Never*. But no one predicted the mass hysteria that trimming off the star's signature swag caused. Bieber's hairstylist, Vanessa Price, calls it the 'Justin Bieber 2011', but some fans have not quite adjusted to his new look. Nearly 80,000 of his fans were so upset, they stopped following him on Twitter!

Shortly after he chopped off his cool coif, Justin tweeted about it. 'yeah so it's true…i got a lil haircut…i like it…and we are giving all the hair cut to CHARITY to auction. Details coming soon…' The supersweet singer gave a lock of his hair to TV show host, Ellen DeGeneres, who auctioned off the sacred strands for $40,668 after 98 bids. All the money will go to The Gentle Barn Foundation, an animal rescue organization.

Liverpool, UK
In March 2011, fans hoping to catch a glimpse of the Biebs made so much noise outside his hotel that fifty police officers had to hold them back. Justin even sent out a plea for quiet on his Twitter feed, so he could go to sleep.

Manchester, UK
Justin couldn't resist playing the pranking older brother when Willow Smith joined him on his UK tour – during one performance of 'Whip My Hair' in March, little Willow was startled when JB and her older brother, Jaden, leaped on stage and started dancing with her. She didn't let them put her off though, and introduced them as her new backing dancers.

Paris, France
In February 2011, police had to shut a shop when fans mobbed the Biebs at a meet-and-greet.

Kuala Lumpur, Malaysia
Fans were so excited about Justin's forthcoming concert in April 2011, that they organized a flashmob, dancing brilliantly to a mash-up of the Bieb's hits.

Tokyo, Japan
Justin stuck to his commitment to complete his tour in Japan, despite a few safety concerns following the earthquake and tsunami there earlier in the year. In May 2011, he finished things off with a spectacular concert in Japan's capital city, announcing on Twitter that he would donate some of the proceeds to the Japanese Red Cross.

Sydney, Australia
At a concert in the city in May 2011, someone threw eggs at the stage, luckily missing the Biebs. But the next day, Justin did have a little egg on his face after disrupting take-off by wandering around. JB apologised to flight attendants and buckled-up.

MAD ABOUT JUSTIN?

Justin's the perfect prince of pop – you're his number one fan, but what would you say to him?

Fill in the lines below by following the instructions or using one of the choices in brackets.

I'm mad about Justin Bieber! He is the most _____ singer in the entire world. I think that he is so cool because of the way he _____ _____ (helps others, sings & dances, jokes around) and the purple _____ (hat, shoes, hoodie) he wears. _____ is my favourite colour. (Your favourite colour)

The coolest thing about Justin is his _____ , and I just love his sweet _____ (songs, smile, dance moves). Nobody can sing like Bieber can!

His best song is _____

_____ (your favourite song), and my favourite music video is _____ (your favourite video).

If I could meet him, I would tell him that I'm his number one fan because I know _____ (number) of his songs by heart, and I think he is the best. I would really like to eat _____ (your fave meal) at my fave restaurant, and then we could go to _____ (a place you love to go) together.

Justin is my idol because _____ _____

One day, I hope I get the chance to meet him. Justin, I _____ (verb) you

JUST THE FACTS

If you want to be a true Belieber, you've got to know the facts! Find out everything there is to know about Justin — from what he loves to his best friends' names and so much more.

Did You Know?

JB loves going to the movies and playing video games.

Quoi? Did you say Justin is bilingual? He can speak English and French!

His worst habit is eating too much candy.

He got to throw the first pitch at a baseball game in the USA, in 2010.

Justin's best friends' names are Christian and Ryan.

In February 2010, a false rumour was spread about Justin that he had died!

Bieber taught himself to play the guitar, piano, trumpet and drums.

Justin has a younger half-brother and half-sister, whose names are Jaxon and Jazmyn.

The Biebs like to draw.

One of his ambitions is to perform a duet with music star Beyoncé.

Justin prefers white bread over brown.

Justin's fave superhero is Superman.

He hates Ugg boots on girls.

He doesn't get nervous when performing in front of thousands of people.

Justin is a daredevil. He even bungee jumped off a bridge while he was in New Zealand.

The Biebs doesn't own a wallet. He just stuffs things in his pockets.

Justin secretly loves the film *The Notebook*.

His hobbies include playing sports, skateboarding and breakdancing.

His fave breakfast food is Cap'n Crunch cereal.

Justin Timberlake offered to sign Bieber, but Usher won Justin's heart in the end.

JB loves golf.

Justin can count to ten in German.

Justin has a tattoo of a bird in flight on his hip. It's a family tradition, and his Dad has one, too.

When Justin was born, singer Celine Dion's 'The Power of Love' was number one on the Billboard charts.

The Biebs is left-handed.

Justin's mum travels with him when he's on the road.

Justin doesn't know the US National Anthem, but can sing the Canadian one in two languages!

The name of Justin's vocal coach is Jan Smith, but he sometimes calls her Mama Jan.

JB had his first kiss at age 13.

His fave TV show is Smallville and his fave movie is Rocky IV.

JB's fave hockey team is the Toronto Maple Leafs of the National Hockey League.

JB has both of his ears pierced.

BEHIND THE MUSIC

You know all the words to every Justin Bieber song. You've got the moves from every video down pat. But do you know the story behind each song? Get the backstage lowdown.

One Time

In the video for the hit song, 'One Time,' Justin takes over Usher's house and throws a fabulous party. Justin got to fly his best friend, Ryan, in to Atlanta so he could be in the video, and Usher even helped out with the production. They all had a blast making the video, and planned on releasing it a few weeks after the single came out. But that's not how it happened!

Somehow, the video got posted on iTunes two weeks before it was supposed to be there! Scooter, Justin's manager (pictured below), was steaming mad at first because the song was there early and no one knew about it. So Justin posted the news on Facebook and Twitter.

A few days later, 'One Time' was the number three song on the iTunes chart.

Down to Earth

Justin wrote the song 'Down to Earth' for his first album, *My World*. He was really excited about it, and it's become a huge fan favourite. Justin likes the song because people can really connect with the emotional lyrics.

Usher told Justin that some songs work best when the singer can really show his true feelings. Justin thinks that this song lets his deep feelings shine through. Bieber also loves that this song 'doesn't need any spectacular stage effects in the touring show; the best thing I can do is just sing it straight from my heart.' He admits, 'Sometimes the emotion of it is enough to bring tears to my eyes.'

One Less Lonely Girl

The video for 'One Less Lonely Girl' has been called 'the musical equivalent of a chick flick'. People have also said it was corny, but Justin disagrees — and so do thousands of fans! In the video, the gorgeous girl who is cast opposite Justin drops a scarf while she's at the Laundromat. Justin then sends her on a truly sweet treasure hunt — complete with sweet notes, PUPPIES and flowers — to get it back.

'I didn't immediately get that they meant it as an insult,' admits Justin. 'They dissed this part where there are some puppies at a pet shop, and I was like "What? Who doesn't like puppies? And more important, who thinks pretending not to like puppies will make them more attractive to girls?"'

Baby

This video, which was shot in a bowling alley, was inspired by one of Justin's musical heroes, Michael Jackson. 'We're kind of going off the "You Make Me Feel" video ... I'm following her around trying to get the girl,' he reveals. And Justin really was chasing the girl! When his beautiful co-star, Jasmine Villegas asked him why he was chasing her around the bowling alley, he answered, 'Because you are just so gorgeous and you have such a stunning personality.'

Not only does Justin know how to charm the ladies, but he also has some sweet moves on the dance floor. In the video, Justin got to show off his moon-walking skills — one of Michael Jackson's signature moves.

WHAT KIND OF FAN ARE YOU?

Call your BFFs and find the perfect accessory to cover up the damage.

Your fave outfit has a stain on it. What do you do?

Raid your wardrobe for the perfect concert-going gear.

Check out some music videos for inspiration and head to the shops.

START HERE
OMG! The Biebs is having a concert in your town. What do you do?

Design an eye-catching poster to take to the show.

Hit the shops so you can glam it up with glitter-glue.

Your poster looks really blah. What do you do?

Add some fab photos of you and the Biebs.

The outfit looks better, but not great. What do you do?

Shrug it off. You just can't wait to see the show.

Accessorize until the stain is undetectable!

Justin's Manager
You could be Justin's manager. You are cool, calm and collected, yet stylish and fun.

Justin is spotted shopping at the store you are in. What do you do?

Nearly faint. His outfit is even cooler in person than you ever imagined.

Start singing your fave Bieber song at the top of your voice.

Bieber Stylist
You love all-things Bieber, especially his super-cute hair and his stunning swag. In addition to a fab fan, you'd make a superb stylist.

Singing Star
You know all the lyrics and every tune there is. You love Justin, but you absolutely adore his music.

Making sure that you and your friends know all the words to all the songs.

It's just minutes to showtime. What are you doing?

Practising all the moves from Justin's latest video.

Dancin' Diva!
You've got all the moves, and you just love the way Justin dances. You're a dreamer just waiting to dance your way to the spotlight one day.

IN THE SPOTLIGHT

It's been quite a journey for Justin, from his very first hit single, to tours across the world and film premieres. Check out some of his biggest moments in the spotlight.

1st March 1994: Little Biebs appears on the scene — born in London, Ontario, Canada.

September 2007: Justin wins third place in the Stratford Idol competition.

October 2008: Justin is officially signed to Island Records.

7th July 2009: Bieber's first single, 'One Time' hits radio airwaves in the USA.

17th November 2009: *My World*, Justin's debut album is released.

22nd December 2009: *My World* sells over one million copies, and Justin is awarded a platinum album disc.

23rd March 2010: Justin's second album, *My World 2.0*, tops the US charts.

28th March 2010: The premiere of Justin's TV show, *The Diary of Justin Bieber* airs on MTV, to give fans a behind-the-scenes peek into his life.

5th April 2010: Justin performs at The White House Easter Egg Roll — an Easter celebration concert.

23rd June 2010: Justin's first headline tour — visiting towns and cities around North America — kicks off in Hartford, Connecticut, USA.

12th October 2010: *Justin Bieber: First Step 2 Forever: My Story*, Justin's memoir, is released.

19th November 2010: *My World 2.0* has sold over 2 million copies. Justin is awarded a double platinum disc.

2nd December 2010: Justin is nominated for two Grammy Awards.

23rd December 2010: The *My World* tour ends in Atlanta, Georgia, USA.

8th February 2011: Hundreds of fans come out to see Justin and his film, *Never Say Never* in 3D at the Los Angeles film premiere.

13th February 2011: Justin hits the red carpet at the Grammys in style. Even though he doesn't win, he's still shining bright.

21st February 2011: Justin cuts his gorgeous trademark hair! But it doesn't stop him looking super-cute.

4th March 2011: Justin kicks off his international *My World* tour in Birmingham, UK.

25th March 2011: Justin contributes his song 'Pray' to *Songs for Japan*, a charity album released today to raise money following the earthquake and tsunami.

27th March 2011: It's a double win for Justin at the Juno Awards in Canada — Pop Album of the Year for *My World 2.0* and the Fan Choice Award.

22nd May 2011: Out of a phenomenal 11 nominations, Justin storms home with six Billboard Awards!

June 2011: Justin launches his own floral fragrance for girls, *Someday.*

BIEBS IN 3D

You've seen him on stage, on countless TV shows and in tons of newspapers and magazines, but this year, Justin Bieber has made it to the big screen in his very own 3D film.

Hollywood Buzz

On 2nd August 2010, not long after he'd told the world he was releasing a memoir, Justin stopped hearts all over the world when he broke the news — he would be starring in his own 3D film all about his rise to fame. The film, which was directed by John M. Chu, was released to the public on 11th February 2011, just in time for Valentine's Day.

Fan Power

Thanks to devoted fans like you, the film, which sees Justin go from small town nobody to filling Madison Square Garden, is already one of the bestselling documentaries of all time. Director John M. Chu admitted that Bieber has such a strong group of fans, he was afraid he might mess up the movie for them.

Reach for the Stars

The Biebs believes that the film has something for everyone, and hopes that it will inspire people, saying 'If you just focus, and keep your dreams in front of you … and never give up — never say never — then anything is possible.'

Fan Phenomenon

Fans couldn't wait to see JB's Hollywood debut. They tweeted, they waited and they rushed to the box office. Justin even encouraged his fans to come out and see his film by spreading the word on Twitter. Hundreds of fans showed Justin their support by going to see the film and tweeting him encouraging messages. And Justin showed his fans how much he loves them by showing up and surprising some of them at movie theatres in the US.

During the Los Angeles premiere, the girls in the audience screamed so loudly, especially during the scenes that Justin was shown performing at concerts, that it felt more like a live performance than a film.

Perfect Premiere

At the film's premiere in Los Angeles, on 8th February 2011, crowds of Beliebers lined the red carpet to wait for the Biebs to arrive. It was also a star-studded event. Usher, Diddy and many others came to support Justin's film debut.

Around the World

Justin didn't have just one premiere, he had quite a few — in Los Angeles, USA, in London, UK, and in Paris, France. Throngs of excited fans joined him on his fabulous nights to catch a glimpse of the Biebs on-screen and off.

Justin was really excited to get to share the experience with his fans. 'we flew 13 hours to make the #allstargame but the French Premiere of #NSN3D was crazy...je t'aime -,' he tweeted.

The Biebs also wants the film to show his fans that they can reach their goals. 'the response around the world to #NEVERSAYNEVER3D is amazing. we want the movie to inspire people to go after their dreams,' tweeted Justin.

ROAD TO THE RED CARPET

There's no time to lose! Your career is on the rise, but you'll have to race to make it to the red carpet first.

How to play

Place a counter for each player on 'start', grab a dice and get going! Take turns to roll the dice and move the number of spaces shown, then follow the instructions on the board.

TIME OUT

Roll a 6 to get out

You forgot to do your homework after your concert.

Head to the time-out zone.

Your first single is being played on the radio!

Roll again.

START

Your YouTube video gets a million hits!

Jump forward 3 spaces.

You get signed to a great label!

Jump forward 1 space.

Your first show is sold-out!

Jump forward 3 spaces.

YOU WIN!

Everyone's taking your photo on the red carpet.

Roll again.

You've been nominated for a ton of awards.

Move forward 3 spaces

Your album is a huge success!

Roll again.

Uh oh. You need to practise your interview skills.

Miss a turn.

Exhausted from an all-day photoshoot.

Go back 1 space.

Everyone wants your autograph.

Jump forward 1 space.

FAN

JB has loads of fabulous fans. Find out what they get up to here.

For the Fans

Justin is so grateful to his wonderful fans — that's you! He knows that without you, he'd never have gotten the chance to be where he is now. 'My dreams used to be a one-in-a-million chance,' he admits. 'I never forget that none of this world would have happened without you.'

Biebs Medicine

Justin loves to serenade his fans on stage when he's performing in a concert. One night, Justin had one of his lovely fans in the spotlight with him. He sang to her and then handed her his hat.

The next day, this lovely fan started chemotherapy — a special treatment for cancer — and she

TASTIC!

was very scared. She went through lots of tests and struggled with her disease, but she says that looking at the pictures of Justin that decorated her hospital room, remembering the hat he'd given her and chatting with the doctors and nurses about all-things Bieber kept her spirits high. When she lost all her hair as a result of the treatment, the fan wore Justin's hat.

The fan, who is now on her way to a long, healthy life, wrote Justin a terrific thank-you letter. 'I'll keep praying for her,' Justin says. 'So many fans I've met along the road have taught me to never forget to Never Say Never.'

The Sweetest Thing

There are Beliebers of all ages and backgrounds. One of the cutest little Biebettes is Cody, who was just three-years-old when she fell for Justin. In a YouTube video that was posted in 2010, little Cody is seen crying because she loves Justin and she can't see him. Not long after, Justin appeared on US TV show, *Jimmy Kimmel Live!* in Los Angeles, where he met Cody backstage. She was thrilled to see him and gave him a big hug. 'Funny thing is,' reveals Justin, 'I was just as excited to meet her.'

You've Got a Friend

Justin's popularity hasn't stopped him remembering how tough things can be for other people. When Casey Heynes, a 15-year-old Australian boy, who has been bullied almost as long as he can remember, stood up to one of his tormentors, he had no idea where it would lead.

The Biebs heard about his story and decided to show Casey some support, bringing him up on stage in Melbourne Australia, and later tweeting that Casey is 'a real life hero'. Aww.

TELL ME

Bieber has a lot to say — from Twitter to interviews all over the world. Here are some of the latest and greatest Bieb-tastic quotes.

'A lot can change in three years ... it's unreal'

'The success I've achieved comes to me from God ...'

'I'm a proud Canadian and I hope that comes through in everything I do'

'No better feeling than coming back home and seeing your grandparents standing there waiting for u. no judgments. pure love'

'My fans are amazing. They will always come to my rescue.'

'My mom is an absolute sweetheart ...'

'What kind of jerk doesn't want love? I bet 95% of sixteen-year-old guys would admit to thinking forty-five girl-related thoughts every three minutes.'

'You have to let yourself do stuff you're not good at'

'One day I noticed the world was full of beautiful girls'

'Music brings people together and that is what I am proudest of'

'I was up in the sky. I was up there among the stars! It was just nuts'

'I want everything to go right. I don't want to let anyone down'

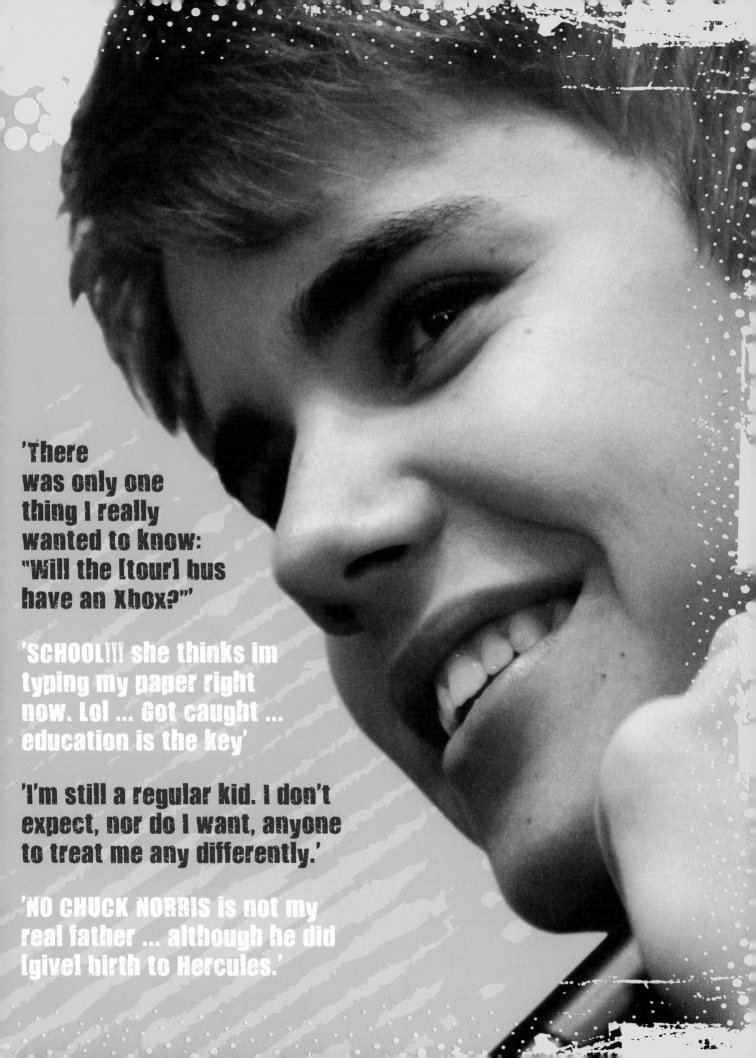

'There was only one thing I really wanted to know: "Will the [tour] bus have an Xbox?"'

'SCHOOL!!! she thinks im typing my paper right now. Lol ... Got caught ... education is the key'

'I'm still a regular kid. I don't expect, nor do I want, anyone to treat me any differently.'

'NO CHUCK NORRIS is not my real father ... although he did [give] birth to Hercules.'

WOULD YOU RATHER?

If you had the chance to meet Justin Bieber, which of these fab things would you choose?

Go on holiday with Justin
OR
Go on tour with Justin?

Bake him your fave cake
OR
Have Justin cook for you?

Hang out with him and his friends
OR
Be in his next video?

Write your own song with Justin
OR
Sing 'Never Say Never' together at the top of your lungs?

Head to the skate park
OR
Learn to play guitar with the Biebs?

Eat ice cream together
OR
Munch popcorn with him at the cinema?

Sing a song together
OR
Show him your sweet dance moves?

Take photos of you together
OR
Attend a photoshoot with the Biebs?

Be his guest at a film premiere
OR
Walk the red carpet as his competition at the Grammys?

Perform with Justin onstage at a concert
OR
Go to the show with VIP, front row tickets?

Take the Biebs to your fave restaurant
OR
Ride your fave roller coaster together?

Go for a ride in a jet with Justin
OR
Take a spin in a limo with him?

BIEBER'S BIRTHDAY BASH

Hundreds of fans wished Justin a happy birthday, but what did he do for the big 1-7? Read on to find out how the Biebs celebrated his special day.

The Perfect Party

He's the youngest male solo artist to top the Billboard chart since Stevie Wonder did it in 1963. He's stood on the red carpets of many major events, including the world-famous Grammy Awards, and his first record has gone double-platinum. By his 17th birthday, Bieber's debut film, *Never Say Never*, had already earned $60 million at the box office. So what did he do to celebrate his birthday?

Belieb it or not, Justin did not have a huge birthday blowout when he turned 17. Justin had only four days to relax between tours, so he want to chill with his grandparents on his special day. Justin reveals, 'My grandma makes the best cheesecake — cherry cheesecake. She made that for my 13th birthday.' No big party plans meant that Justin was able to celebrate 17 exactly how he wanted to — just relaxing with his family before heading back out on the road. Now that's a perfect party!

Birthday Wishes

His 17th birthday may not have been a major event, but it was a big day for his fans. Hundreds of them posted their wishes for a happy birthday to Justin on Twitter and Facebook. Some even made YouTube videos, which they posted online, to share with their favourite star. Justin tweeted, 'thank u ... and ...great bday. flew in grandma and got my cake. hung out with friends. got surprised.'

Party Planner

Justin didn't have a big party this year, but what would you have planned to make his 17th birthday the best party ever? Use the space below to share what you would have done.

kiss him in vite

evrey boddy have a

great time. Love Aoife

MARY HIM.

the end

The End

THE ULTIMATE FAN QUIZ

So you think you know all there is about Justin Bieber? Test your knowledge to find out if you're really the ultimate fan. The answers are on page 61.

1. On Justin's first date, what dish did he spill on his shirt?

a. Pasta carbonara   b. Spaghetti bolognaise   c. Pea soup

---

2. The Biebs' first headlining tour was called:

a. My World Tour   b. My World 2.0 Tour   c. Justin Bieber Tour

---

3. Which of these stars has Justin not admitted to having a crush on?

a. Kim Kardashian   b. Beyoncé   c. Gwen Stefani

4. Justin was discovered on this popular website:

a. Twitter   b. YouTube   c. Facebook

5. In which city was Justin's hat snatched by excited fans?

a. Auckland, New Zealand
b. New York, USA
c. London, United Kingdom

6. Who is Justin's manager?

a. Usher
b. Jay-Z
c. Scooter Braun

7. How old was Justin when he started playing the drums?

a. 10
b. 6
c. 2

8. Which of these instruments does Justin not play?

a. Banjo
b. Trumpet
c. Piano

9. Justin's middle name is:

a. Drew
b. Edward
c. Andrew

10. The Biebs' concert at Madison Square Garden sold out in:

a. 22 minutes
b. 22 hours
c. 22 days

11. Which of these stars shares JB's birthday?

a. Lady Gaga
b. Ke$ha
c. Selena Gomez

12. One day, Justin would like to be:

a. An architect
b. A drama teacher
c. A radio talk show host

BORN TO BE SOMEBODY

At 17 years old, he's already super-successful. But what are Justin's plans for the future?

Stay in the Spotlight

Justin is loving his life on stage, on tour and in the spotlight. He's enjoying connecting with his fans, and has no plans to leave the music biz anytime soon. But music isn't the only thing Justin is interested in.

After making his own film, Justin would like to act in other roles. 'I'm gonna start doing more movies — start getting more scripts and start finding some things that I really wanna do,' he promises. He's even getting some help looking through scripts from Jaden and Willow Smith's dad, actor, Will Smith.

Manager Scooter Braun also revealed that Justin is hoping to get to act alongside comic actor, Will Ferrell.

The Next Michael Jackson?

It's no secret that Michael Jackson is someone who inspired Justin's music and dance style, and Justin and his team think that he could be the next MJ.

'Michael was so amazing. He worked so hard and knew how to manage his career. He's someone I look up to,' Justin reveals.

Smart Move!

Justin isn't just a brilliant singer and dancer, he's also quite good at his studies. With nearly perfect grades, Justin hopes that he will be able to use his talents off-stage by attending university. Justin says, 'I always travel with a private tutor who I have five three-hour sessions a week with. I want to finish high school and also college and then evolve wherever my music takes me.'

Up!

No matter what happens in the future, one thing is for sure, Justin Bieber is only getting started in his successful journey. And he knows he couldn't have made it this far without his family, friends, fans and his dreams. 'Follow your dreams,' he says. 'You can do anything you set your mind to.' There's no stopping this star as he shoots to the top!

ALL THE ANSWERS

Never Say ... (pages 12–13)

1. Justin Bieber 2. Miranda Cosgrove 3. Justin Bieber 4. Justin Bieber 5. Sean Kingston 6. Taylor Swift 7. Katy Perry 8. Justin Bieber 9. Ellen DeGeneres 10. Justin Bieber

My Words (page 18)

Z	Y	G	O	S	O	S	B	F	G	J	Y	U	D	P
E	M	C	F	E	T	E	E	M	J	É	S	S	B	L
U	M	C	I	Q	V	R	L	L	Q	L	J	M	Y	F
S	A	G	Y	O	S	T	A	P	E	O	X	B	H	
A	R	P	N	E	J	J	E	T	Y	N	E	L	C	
T	G	C	D	Z	N	H	L	G	F	G	A	E	B	O
H	É	R	E	T	T	I	W	T	A	8	I	N	J	O
Z	C	G	F	É	H	O	Q	B	L	Z	R	P	C	W
Q	S	D	Z	O	I	O	H	S	L	P	R	B	I	Q
L	Q	H	V	B	N	N	O	X	C	A	Z	J	W	V
D	O	P	Z	X	P	H	N	N	Y	O	K	I	H	Y
F	B	W	B	Q	Q	T	U	F	P	B	Q	R	W	D
Z	H	Z	J	R	E	L	L	I	R	H	T	É	M	
I	U	T	L	Q	I	W	F	F	F	O	H	T	E	M
Q	T	L	J	C	G	P	H	M	Q	Y	X	U	O	R

Guess Who! (page 34)

1. False: actress Jessica Biel asked for $5,000; Justin hoped to raise $10,000 — and he did!

2. True: Justin Bieber and Ozzy Osbourne auctioned off the space suits they wore in a TV advert in 2011. The money they raised went to a cancer charity.

3. True: Justin donated the money to the Community Foundation of Middle Tennessee's Nashville Flood Fund.

4. False: Oprah Winfrey signed the bone.

5. False: singer Bono helped to start this organization.

6. True.

7. False: author J. K. Rowling hand wrote a history of one of the Harry Potter characters to raise money for Book Aid International.

8. True.

9. True.

10. False: Miley Cyrus donated a bag that she decorated.

The Ultimate Fan Quiz (pages 56–57)

1. b – Spaghetti bolognaise 2. a – *My World Tour* 3. c – Gwen Stefani 4. b – YouTube 5. a – Auckland, New Zealand 6. c – Scooter Braun 7. c – 2 8. a – Banjo 9. a – Drew 10. a – 22 minutes 11. b – Ke$ha 12. a – An architect